GRANMA'S BOOK OF TRUTHS

Remember

GRANMA'S BOOK OF TRUTHS

How to Live In Truth With Your Child To Keep Their Mind, Body & Soul Strong And Prepare Them For Life.

Remember

LINDA M NOON

Copyright © 2023 Linda M Noon

First Paperback Edition

First published in AUSTRALIA 2023

All rights reserved. No part of this publication can be reproduced, stored in a retrieval system or transmitted in any form or by any means, electronic, mechanical, photocopying, recording or otherwise, without prior permission of the publishers and copyright holders.

The moral rights of the author have been asserted.

Cover illustration by Unknown from Facebook

GRANMA'S BOOK OF TRUTHS
ISBN: 978-0-9874621-9-0

A catalogue record for this book is available from the National Library of Australia.

Typeset in Cambria, Times New Roman, and Courier New.

Printed and designed in Australia.

Editing, Formatting & Design:
Michael Young

AVA ORION Media
Melbourne, Australia

www.AvaOrionMedia.com

Dedication

This book is dedicated to:

My Grandchildren and all Children to come. To all the Children of the World.
In the hope of enabling them to see the Truth of what the World is about and how to maneuver between life's ups and downs with some knowledge of choices, responsibility, action and Love.

Thank you to them all for being a huge part of my life and the inspiration for this book. I wish I had known what these pages contain much earlier in my life's journey. I would have been able to have made better informed choices as I was growing up, instead of finding out the hard way, during these turbulent times of the Covid pandemic (plan-demic) 2020-2023.

Thank you to my family and friends for supporting me even though they think I am crazy most of the time.

Thank you to my editor Michael Young for helping me bring this book into physical manifestation. Along with my previous two books Tilly's Journey to Fairy Kingdom & Awakening of the Lotus on Lulu.com

Remember

Table of Contents

Introduction 1

Granma's Book Of Truths 5

    We All Make Mistakes 7

    Illusion 9

    Deception 11

    Indoctrination. 13

    Health. 17

    Propaganda 21

    Ancestors 39

    The Passage Of Time 41

    Food For Thought 45

    Open Your Mind 47

More Truths I Have Remembered 63

Bibliography 79

Acknowledgements 83

About The Author 85

Introduction

Congratulations on purchasing my book and Thank You.

Linda M Noon

Clinical Hypnotherapist.Dip.Clin 2003

Meditation Teacher 1999

Reiki Master/Teacher 1998

Buddhist Philosophy & Meditation 2000

Author

I am a Mother and now a Grandmother. Upon watching my Grandchildren and seeing them trying to find their way through life, the brain washing of Social Media and Schools even through seeing what are supposed to be innocent children's shows like Pepper Pig, Lava Island and other children's shows, I saw subliminal messages being forced upon their developing minds through the **tell-lies-vision** (television).

I saw Pepper Pig wearing masks and talking about Covid, they even dubbed over the voices with another voice to get the message across. I saw A bug on Lava Island, the last 3 mins in, masturbating after it fell in love with another bug it rescued. I tried to contact Netflix about it but I could only live chat with them, there was nowhere to send an email or ring them up. They assured me that my complaint would be sent to the correct department. I never received a Ref number or email about my complaint. I saw all of this because those were the shows my Grandchildren were watching and I had no idea, I just thought they are Children's shows, what harm could they cause? They caused fear about Covid and catching a deadly virus to the Children. I saw the sexualization begin, through what was supposed to be innocent child cartoons.

The purpose of this book is to bring awareness to the youth and the upcoming generations who are the future of our Planet.

I write this book as a go-to for them to think about and hopefully research for themselves. Instead of blindly following or believing anything that comes out of the Mainstream Media (MSM), Social Media, Schools, Government, or TV shows.

I give them food for thought and encouragement to be their own person in a loving, respectful way.

No one has to believe what I write in these pages, all I ask is that you keep an open mind and research for yourself. Don't take my word alone for it. Knowledge is Power.

There are many new platforms now, besides Google, TikTok, Twitter, Instagram, Newspapers etc. where you can research for yourself. The above are designed to give you information on *their* narrative.

Here are some of the Truth sources and I'm sure there are many more: Rumble.com, Bitchute.com, YouTube, NewTube, GB News (Neil Oliver), Christine

Anderson - Politician in the EU for Germany, Andrew Bridgen - England, Senator Alex Antic - South Australia, Senator Babet - Politician in Victoria, Senator Malcolm Roberts in Queensland plus many others who may come after them. Worldwide Health Alliance made up of many Doctors who were silenced during the Pandemic. Dr Mark Hobart here in Victoria was one of many. Dr Dolores Cahill - Ireland, Dr Peter McCullough - America, Dr Robert Malone - America. So many. I also followed Jacquie Dundee for her vast knowledge about the Australian Constitution.

I followed many others that turned out to be red herrings, some wasted time but not for long, though still a lesson. It taught me to be able to pick out the wheat from the chaff using my intuition and **real eyes** (realize), it helped to sharpen my senses and research into them even more, then I could leave them behind.

I use DuckDuckGo as my search engine, it doesn't follow you about or keep your browsing history. So much is censored through Google, which will give you the opposite of the truth.

Don't let the Children wander through life with their heads in the clouds or buried obsessively in their devices. Don't let yourself wander through life oblivious to what is going on around you.

Linda M Noon

Remember

Granma's Book Of Truths

Remember you are loved, always.

Remember you are Love, you are a soul having a human experience.

Remember every thought, feeling, decision and action is entirely your CHOICE.

Remember to choose Love every time, this is your responsibility and no one else's.

Remember it is EASY to be negative or bad, this is your choice too.

Remember it is harder to be positive and good but making this choice builds strength, integrity and good character.

Remember to go within and meditate upon stillness of mind.

Remember everything, all your answers are already within you.

Remember you are a creator & you can choose to create Love, Peace & Inner Balance.

Remember when your thoughts & feelings are in balance, your whole life is in balance and your inner strength will shine through with Love, Health and Compassion.

Remember who and how Powerful you are!

Linda M Noon

We All Make Mistakes

Remember that when you make a mistake it's okay, that is how we learn and we learn not to make the same mistakes.

Remember to forgive yourself for your mistakes and own them.

Remember not to blame others for your mistakes, they were your choices.

Remember not to be impulsive as this can lead to mistakes without thinking.

Remember when you realize you've made a mistake to learn and move on from it.

Remember you always have a choice.

Remember your choices do not always only affect you, there may be others involved.

Remember to align with your heart before making a choice.

Remember if it does not feel right, do not do it.

Remember to be a leader and not a follower.

Remember your inner strength.

Remember to believe in yourself.

Remember you are the master of your own mind.

Remember to apologise for your mistakes.

Remember to forgive your mistakes and more on.

Linda M Noon

Remember

Illusion

Remember not everything is as it appears.

Remember nothing is real.

Remember we are Energy, Frequency and Vibration.

Remember everything is Energy, Frequency and Vibration.

Remember to keep your vibration high, through stillness meditation, healthy diet and fresh clean water.

Remember when your vibration is high you are naturally protected from lower vibrations.

Remember that how you see your world is not the same for every other sentient being.

Remember that your thoughts carry a vibration, so keep them positive.

Remember FEAR is False Evidence Appearing Real.

Remember if someone cuts you off in traffic, they could be having a really bad day.

Remember if someone is mean to you, that is a reflection upon them, not you.

Linda M Noon

Remember

Deception

Remember not everyone will love or like you, but that is okay, just stay true to yourself.

Remember there is a saying, be careful of a "Wolf in Sheep's Clothing" meaning someone acting nice to your face but nasty behind your back.

Remember there are people who may be Jealous of you and may want to do harm, but their Jealousy is because they want to have what you have, they must find happiness within themselves.

Remember true Love is measured by a person's actions and not by their words.

Remember when someone truly loves you, you will know it by what they do and not by what they say.

Remember to remain centered in your inner peace, no one can take that away from you, unless you allow it.

Remember for the many that Love you, the same amount may try to use you and mistakenly take your Loving nature as a weakness. Your Loving nature is not a weakness but a Mighty Strength.

Remember do not believe everything that you hear, always do your own research.

Remember do not believe everything that you see on Social Media and Television (Tell-Lies-Vision).

Linda M Noon

Remember

Indoctrination

Remember when you go to school you are taught only what the Government wants you to learn.

Remember that you are being indoctrinated into a society from a very early age, to not think for yourself, sit down, be quiet and memorise what they are teaching you.

Remember you do not have to follow along and learn what they want you to learn.

Remember what you are being taught is not how to live and survive in this world but how to fit into their society as slaves.

Remember that most of History is a lie, there are many things in history that we have never been told. Like, why no one is allowed in Antarctica and why are there many truths hidden under the Vatican.

Remember that History is usually in favour of white man's success and his wars, bullying, stealing, killing and conquering other countries, stealing what is not rightfully theirs for power, control and greed. Like all the countries belonging to the Commonwealth. (Crown)

Remember the education departments are trying to enforce Gender Pronouns onto the sexes.

Remember they now want Drag Queens to read to our little ones in libraries and schools to cause confusion, to emasculate our males. What has this to do with education?

Remember that parents can be jailed or fined $10,000 if they won't let their child choose his or her own sex.

Remember that if you are born a male or a female you cannot biologically change your sex. (DNA)

Remember they say you can Identify as what you like, just by how you think and feel. How does that make sense?

Remember that as you grow and mature your thoughts and feelings can naturally change. You can identify as much as you like with whatever you like, but it will not change a biological fact.

Remember your Sexual Preference does not matter, what matters is, it should not be enforced upon any other living being by our Governments.

Remember that there are adult males in our world who want to have sexual relations with children, they want the age of consent reduced, so they will be accepted by society as normal but what about the small child who knows nothing about sexual relations, especially with their tiny bodies.

Remember men dressing up and identifying as women (transgender) want to be allowed to go into a woman's private space, like toilets, changing rooms and female sport. Yet woman transitioning to male are usually not asking to go into the men's toilets, changing rooms or sports. Why is that, is it because they know they are at a disadvantage and male toilets usually smell?

Remember that schools are not teaching the students how to manage money, how to survive the real world outside of education.

Remember your parents pay for you to attend school, college and then you may pay for university. More teachings of memorise and repeat. Like a monkey. After all of that you get a good paying job and pay the Government money with your taxes, until you retire or die.

Remember the Government are in it for themselves.

Remember you are plugged into the Matrix, a robotic slave, that is, until you learn to escape it, by not falling for all their lies and indoctrination.

Remember Children are being deliberately sexualised and brain washed also by Social Media.

Remember Gender confusion is now being taught at School. Some Schools are Teaching without Parental consent. Especially in Europe.

Remember Children are not as social as they used to be.

Remember a Child's freedom is slowly being stripped away from them.

Remember to do what you love and do it with all of your heart, whether that is sport, music etc. Make a good living for yourself.

Remember

Health

Remember to remain as healthy as you can, good healthy diet, exercise, filtered water and grow your own food, possibly under cover (a greenhouse) to keep the toxins out of the soil.

Remember the Health Industry and Big Pharma don't make money off you if you are healthy.

Remember to take organic supplements like NAC, Moringa, Zeolite, Vitamins C, D and Zinc.

Remember we have access to Lifewave Stem Cell activation patches, which activate your Copper peptides. A great protective energy, for within and around you.

Remember to only consume fast food occasionally.

Remember to keep away from fluoride, sugar and high acid foods.

Remember to drink filtered water and drink from glass or Copper bottles.

Remember processed foods and microwave cooking are extremely toxic.

Remember to eat less meat, as it is high in acid, meat is low vibration food because the animals know they are going to be killed and they also want to live. Cancer loves acids and sugars.

Eat freshly caught fish as farmed fish are full of mites and anti-biotics not fit for human consumption.

Remember the vaccinations today are mRNA, Spike Proteins and Graphene Oxide. Highly dangerous.

Remember when the Covid-19 vaccines came out in 2021 they said they will save you, they will stop you catching and spreading Covid-19. Today in 2023, they admit the vaccines do not do any of those things. The new Vaccines are the world's largest experimental vaccine trial, ever. Many millions of deaths occurred worldwide because of them and millions more vaccine injuries.

Remember that even though they have admitted they do not work, they, the Government and the WHO (World Health Organisation), are still pushing them onto the public Worldwide.

Remember when the Covid-19 first appeared throughout the World, millions of elderly worldwide died in nursing homes, not because of Covid-19 but because the World Economic Forum in Davos, headed by self-appointed Klaus Schwab and his crew and our Governments treated the elderly with large amounts of end of life drugs, like Midazolam and Morphine. To cull the elderly. Then falsely recorded their deaths as Covid-19.

Remember the coercion of making people take at least two vaccines or lose your job. Many people took them because they needed money to live, for their young families etc.

Remember when those who refused lost their jobs, homes and families. They were also locked out of shops, restaurants, pubs, clubs, hospitals, Dentists and Doctor's surgeries, I myself included.

Remember Medicare took a tumble, most Doctors no longer bulk bill, medications are in short supply for many people.

Remember when they said you couldn't catch Covid-19 if you were vaccinated.

Remember Covid-19 was never isolated, therefore does not really exist.

Remember when the Hospitals cancelled lifesaving surgeries and refused surgeries if you were not vaccinated, resulting in many lives lost.

All of this can be found, all you have to do is research. There are court cases going on around the World as I write, for crimes against humanity.

Linda M Noon

Propaganda

Remember when they said wearing a mask was a waste of a good mask. (Daniel Andrews - Victorian Premier)

Remember when they then changed their minds and said you must wear a mask, they save lives.

Remember when they made all the Children at school wear a mask and they could hardly breathe, after breathing in their own toxic carbon dioxide making them sick.

Remember when they closed the schools and parents had to do home schooling.

Remember when they said you could not catch the virus outside because it could not survive in the open air.

Remember when they then closed all the parks and you were only allowed outside for 1 hour a day.

Remember when you weren't allowed out at nighttime unless you had a permit to travel to and from work.

Remember when they said that you can have Covid-19 even if you were asymptomatic (no symptoms).

Remember when you could sit outside to eat a meal as long as you were wearing a mask but then you could remove it to eat.

Remember when they put up a ring of steel around Melbourne and no one was allowed to travel more than 5 kilometers from their home, if you were caught you faced a $1,800 fine.

Remember when the Helicopters were flying really low every single night looking for "criminals" who broke the Covid-19 curfew rules.

Remember when you could only go out if you had a partner on the other side of town, to visit them.

Remember when, throughout the whole farce, people could still visit a Brothel (prostitute parlors). During this "deadly pandemic" you could still visit a prostitute.

Remember when you could not get onto a plane unless you had a vaccination pass.

Remember when you had to have a PCR test at the testing sites even though they knew that the test could not differentiate between a Cold, Flu or Covid-19.

Remember when they bought millions of home testing PCR kits when they knew the guy who invented them, Kary Mullis, said they are not designed for this, it will not show Covid-19 and he wanted to sit down with Dr Fauci and have a debate. Strangely, Kary unfortunately died before that could take place.

Remember when the people began to stand up against it all to attend peaceful protests in Melbourne and the Police shot people with Rubber Bullets.

Remember when Police on horseback kettled people in the streets of Melbourne and were firing smoke bombs that made a loud explosive noise and pepper spraying everyone.

Remember when women and children in abusive homes were forced to stay home with their abuser and it got so bad that they had to create help lines for the Children, they were inundated with calls for help and could not cope.

Remember when we had health record privacy except during Covid-19 where you had to disclose your vaccination status and all jobs that were advertised specified that to apply for the job you had to be vaccinated.

Remember when a popular and highly respected Doctor came on TV and spoke of her and her partner having adverse side effects from the vaccines and she has not been interviewed since.

Remember when they threatened Doctors with a $10,000 fine and deregistration if they prescribed Ivermectin, a known and previously approved drug that produced amazing results. The media set about discrediting it as a treatment.

Remember when Clive Palmer bought 33 million doses of Hydroxychloroquine Sulphate to donate to the Australian Government to effectively treat Covid-19 symptoms, but the government then banned Doctors from prescribing it as an option for C19 positive patients.

Remember when they arrested and deregistered Doctors for giving valid exemptions from the vaccine. Dr Mark Hobart and Dr Bay come to mind.

Remember when Surgeons, Nurses and Doctors were making TikTok dancing videos on the empty wards that were supposed to be packed out with the dying people from Covid-19.

Remember when air line Pilots were doing the same Tiktok dancing videos. Highly choreographed.

Remember when small businesses folded and many lost their lively hoods.

Remember when we then had floods in Lismore, far north NSW, and people were being arrested for helping save lives because they were not vaccinated. Some had their bank accounts frozen!

Remember when you could follow the flight paths of planes up North and in Victoria that were suspected of releasing chem trails to make it rain week after week.

Remember when there were no flights around the World but if one went onto the flight path app there were hundreds of planes in the skies.

Remember when all the toilet paper was sold out in the supermarkets and there were some food shortages. People were fighting over toilet paper, so they limited them to two packets each.

Remember when absolutely nothing made any sense and still doesn't.

Remember when we were all in lock down and they started erecting the 5G towers and doing late night road works.

Remember when they started to bring out digital currency, facial recognition cameras, QR coding and want us to order food at a table using a QR code and a robot brings your food to your table.

Remember how they now make us go through self-serve and use your bank card with minimal staff on a check out and most self-serve are card only.

Remember how, in the months of April and May of 2023 they have now come out on MSM and said that Covid-19 is nothing but a flu and we are all to treat it as such.

Remember how, WHO (World Health Organisation) have also recently said the Covid-19 emergency is now over.

Remember how, they said that the Covid-19 vaccination is not recommended for young children or healthy young people, but they are still pushing it on to older people. In fact, they now have a two in one, Flu and Covid-19.

Remember how, they told young people that they could potentially kill their Granny if they go to visit her, especially if they are unvaccinated.

Remember how families could not visit on Mothers Day and Christmas Day.

Remember how, no one could visit their elderly parents in nursing homes and could only see them through a window and many died scared and alone. The families could also watch them take their last breath on FaceTime.

Remember how the Government tried to make it an offence if people did letter box drops to get the truth out there.

Remember how the Government wanted neighbours to report (dob in) their neighbours if they broke the curfew or had visitors.

Remember how only 5 people could go to a Funeral and sit masked up and over a metre apart.

Remember pregnant Women had to give birth alone without their partner present.

Remember how many young athletes died on the fields Worldwide after vaccines and many suffering Pericarditis, Myocarditis, blood clots and other side effects.

Remember when they took 200 Students by coach to a stadium in NSW to be coerced under Brad Hazzard's instructions to take the vaccine, there was a big screen in the stadium telling them why they need to get the lifesaving vaccine. Some passed out, there was rumor some died but unconfirmed and Brad Hazzard said at a TV conference, "...so what, some fainted, get on with it." He conveniently retired when the Truth began to come out. Brett Sutton also disappeared, the CHO (Chief Health Officer).

Remember how Greg Hunt said, "This is the world's largest clinical vaccination trial of its kind."

Remember when the Media and the Government deliberately lied to us for over two years, to control us through fear, by endlessly reporting the numbers of people dying WITH Covid in their system as having died OF Covid, when they actually died of other causes.

Remember how flu disappeared for the last two years then suddenly made a comeback this year 2023.

Remember how the RBA put interest rates up 12 times in the last 12 months.

Remember how they came up with a Climate Crisis then suddenly changed the wording to Climate Change.

Remember how Electricity, Gas, Fuel and Food prices increased dramatically.

Remember how a war broke out 2021 between Ukraine (Zelensky) and Russia (Putin) and the Western World leapt to Zelensky's defense giving him Billions, Weapons and Tanks.

Remember how Ukraine are not our Allies nor do they belong to NATO.

Remember how Britain, America and Australia gave Zelensky everything he wanted, then Australia was threatened by China.

Remember how Australia is far from a match with China.

Remember Australia has struck an AUKUS deal and America are sending Subs here to help protect our land from a possible Chinese attack.

Remember how there is a war going on and Zelensky has been visited by so many stars in a war zone; Angelina Jolie, Sean Penn. Sean took him an Oscar award as a gift, mind you Zelensky is supposed to be an ACTOR. World leaders, also visited, yet not one of them was wearing a protective vest. I found that strange.

Remember how Bill Gates has been buying up vast amounts of farmland in America and farmers are being targeted in Europe.

Remember how Bill Gates said we can eat Bugs and it will now be added into our foods and they don't even have to include it in the ingredients of the packets. In bread, pasta, cereals, flour etc.

Remember how local Councils have joined the 20 minute neighbourhoods, where everything, including your place of employment, will be within your 20 minute zone. Calling it the Loop.

Remember the 20 minute cities are happening with 26 other countries signing up for it. It has already begun in the UK where you can only leave your area 100 times a year and you have to apply for a permit to do so or receive a fine.

Remember they want us to drive electric cars, where the lithium and cobalt is mined by young children, when they could easily use Hemp. If they really cared, they would use Hemp.

Remember, HOW are they going to dispose of the batteries used by the cars, under the guise of saving the planet?

Remember it is all about control and money. Who can afford to buy an electric car with the way the economy is right now.

Remember we were never supplied with Bio-hazard bins to dispose of the masks when it was such a deadly Virus, instead they ended up in the oceans, killing and maiming marine life.

Remember the hospitals were paid thousands of dollars for every death they listed as Covid-19, no autopsy required. Even if you were hit by a bus.

Remember the 24 hour constant Covid-19 statistics bombarded at us relentlessly, the horrific footage shown, knowing your mind is very powerful and what you believe is true, the biology of belief, although far from the TRUTH.

Granma's Book of Truths

Remember when people went for the test and if positive you had to stay at home and they were sending the army door knocking to make sure you were home in isolation.

Remember all the supermarkets and big stores had markers on the floor, we had to stand 1 metre apart.

Remember when you were allowed out for dinner and you would be greeted with a staff members proudly wearing a Covid Marshal Badge.

Remember being discriminated against if you were unvaccinated or refused service if you weren't wearing a mask, although you had a legal exemption certificate from your Doctor.

Remember being made to sit in your car in the Doctor's carpark until a member of staff came out to tell you to come in.

Remember when all we had to say as a collective was NO. That didn't happen.

Remember how helpless, scared and desperate it made people feel.

Remember how being vaccinated or not tore families apart even to this day.

Remember how many committed suicide because they were so scared and many lost everything.

Remember that the FDA and TGA never tested the safety of the vaccine but just took the word of a Pfizer report.

Remember how this Pandemic was supposed to have taken place in 2016, the Great Reset.

Remember the WHO want a One World Government and a NWO (New World Order).

Remember how our Governments went along with it, but never followed the rules themselves.

Remember how Daniel Andrews recently visited China in 2023 in private, no media allowed, after all China's threats, to grovel and strike a deal with China to allow Thousands of Students to return to study in Australia. When asked at a conference what his trip was about his reply was, "Look, it's not about me or you, it's about the future of Victoria."

Remember when Daniel Andrew's was caught not wearing a mask.

Remember when Daniel Andrews was offering all the Children a free show bag if they got vaccinated and the posters outside of the Chemists were of an enchanted forest to attract the Children, a bit like the Piped Piper. Now 2023, the vaccine is not recommended for the young and healthy.

Remember when they were coercing pregnant women to get vaccinated.

Remember when they laid off Nurses and Health Care Workers for choosing body autonomy, now the Government are advertising for hundreds to come from overseas with the promise of making it easier if they wish to become a permanent resident. Not forgetting the Government are offering cash incentives to Australians to train up to become a Nurse. Vaccinated of course.

Remember when the Government enforced the mandates, then passed it over to Employers to enforce because the Government said, "We can't force anyone to get vaccinated."

Remember the Government instructed the Employers to keep a record of all the Mandates and the Employer had to notify the Government at set times about their staff's vaccine status. The Government hand balled it to the Employers, is that so the Government cannot be held liable.

Remember the Government are now telling Employers that all of the staff vaccine records had to be destroyed by August 2023 but some Employers were still requiring new staff to be vaccinated, figure that one out, doesn't make sense if they had to be destroyed by August 2023.

Remember the Government want to inject livestock with the mRNA and Bill Gates has been experimenting with injecting Avocados and Tomatoes with the mRNA.

Remember in Victoria we had the strictest lockdowns and mandates.

Remember how the MSM bombarded us relentlessly with this highly contagious deadly virus and at the same time, bombarded us with Floods, Food Shortages, mini Earthquakes, increasing Utility Bills, increasing Interest Rates, increasing Fuel and Grocery bills, Wars and Job losses.

Remember the amount of people that lost their homes and had no choice but to live in their cars.

Remember how the Police arrested anyone who spoke out under Common Law instead of Maritime Law.

Remember how we discovered that the Government of 1986 introduced a fictious non-existent "Queen of Australia." Changed the seal of the Commonwealth to depict an Emu and a Kangaroo instead of Her Majesty the Queen's seal. The Commonwealth fraudulently gave themselves the power to sell off our Commonwealth Estate.

Remember our Government and Police Force is a registered Private Corporation in the USA. It is a Business. In 1974 they registered with the American Securities Exchange Commission.

Remember 1993-1995 the Government signed off on hundreds of agreements written into Agenda 21/Agenda 2030 complete with a Planetary Depopulation Genocide program including mandatory vaccinations, a 267 page document written in 1967 by Henry Kissinger.

Remember that when you are born your parents must register you with the Births, Deaths and Marriages Registrar. Unknowingly, your parents are signing you over to the Government and your Birth Certificate then makes tremendous amounts of money on the Stocks and Shares market, not for you but for them.

Remember Children are not taught about Common Law in School and it is extremely hard to enforce Common Law as our Government no longer goes by it unless it suits them. They go by Maritime Law, which means the stricter law out at sea.

Remember under Common Law you do not have to pay taxes, yet the Government take it straight from your earnings, nor are you required to register your car.

Remember in 1990s a suppression order was placed by the Royal Commission containing the names of 28 Political, Judicial and High Profile figures allegedly connected to Pedophilia.

Remember the Government are supposed to work for the People, but it is the other way around. How did that happen?

Remember all the promises our Prime Ministers and MPs make before an election, then break all of them.

Remember Mandates and Directions are not Laws.

Remember Digital Identification and Facial Recognition are being implemented at great speed around the World.

Remember QR coding to tap in everywhere, so your every move is tracked and traced.

Remember huge cyber hacks on Banks, Medibank and mobile providers, stealing all your private information and the hackers were asking for ransoms.

Remember how, when you think you are having a private conversation and it may be about an item you would like to purchase, all of a sudden when you sign-in to your Social Media the first newsfeed is about the item you have been discussing.

Remember how your mobile device tracks your locations through Google maps and then asks you for a review on where you have been.

Remember Maui, Fires, DEW (Directed Energy Weapons), Land grab, 15 Minute Cities.

Remember the Maui Fires 8-11 August 2023 yet a book had already appeared on Amazon called Fire & Fury, Published on the 10 August 2023 about the harrowing experiences of the People who lived through the fire. Within that two days prior to publishing "Dr Miles Stone" had all of this information. That is rather amazing since no one could enter or leave, no food, no water, no petrol. Where were the choppers to drop supplies.

Remember AI (Artificial Intelligence) is emerging at a rapid rate right now. AI could write a book within 2 hours or less.

Remember MSM reported the flames were so hot, it melted steel but tar on the roads were okay. Trees were still standing. They are pumping Climate Change.

Remember all is not as it seems. Nothing is real.

Remember if you survived all of this, you are an incredible human being!

Linda M Noon

Ancestors

Remember to honour your Ancestors, it took a thousand loves for you to be here.

Remember your Ancestors fought in WWI and WWII so that you may benefit from the sacrifices that each one of them made for your Freedom.

Remember many Soldiers never returned to their families or homeland. During those times many MEN were sacrificed in the name of Country.

Remember your Ancestors did not fight for you to decide which latest phone or fashion you want to own.

Remember your Ancestors who fought and died for you, the Future. They loved you before you were born.

Remember your Ancestors Loved their Country and Freedom too.

Remember your Ancestors were also lied to, to get them join the Wars, believing they were doing it for all of the right reasons and if they didn't join of their own free will they were conscripted (forced).

Remember your Ancestors were merely Children themselves, some even lied about their age to join up, selflessly serving.

Remember your Ancestors of eons of time gone by, for they too made many sacrifices, and you made it here today, in their far away future.

Remember you carry within your DNA all the Love, Knowledge, Truth and Wisdom from your Ancestors.

Remember your Ancestors struggled for many years in poverty after the Wars and were not looked after when those who survived returned home.

Remember there were many other Wars too in the past; Vietnam, Korea, Iran, Iraq, Afghanistan, Syria and so on. More recently in Israel and Palestine. There has never been much peace in the World. This has been deliberately contrived to divide and control though fear. Usually headed by the USA.

Remember your Ancestors also fought hundreds of years prior. So much killing, pillaging and conquering, enforcing false beliefs for complete control, power and greed.

Remember

The Passage Of Time

Remember to go back to the beginning, God is a Frequency and vibration which equates to Love, not an old man sat on a thrown up in sky. God is not religion. Look at Sumeria, Anunnaki, Atlantis, Lemuria, the Emerald Tablets of Thoth and Egypt. Enki & Enlil. Buddha, Krishna, Jesus and Hermes.

Remember they removed pages from the bible. Gospel of Thomas.

Remember Jesus taught that which Thoth had been teaching 35,000 years prior to Jesus Christ.

Remember the Pyramids were not built in the way MSM, Education or Books tell you.

Remember all humans are Hybrid, it is in your DNA. 450,000 years ago and beyond.

Remember there have been many, many before us, they came to teach us of the truth. Many civilisations left text, hieroglyphs and many mysterious complicated architectural buildings and Pyramids scattered around the World, with messages of what was taking place, far back in the distant past of what we know as time.

Remember a Belief is not a Truth, as beliefs can and do change, like Father Christmas and the Tooth Fairy, as you mature and grow. A TRUTH can never be changed.

Remember there are many timelines all playing out at the same time, past, present and future.

Remember there are fragments of Truth in what we call Holy scriptures, but not the whole Truth, they have been manipulated, added and removed by man to fit into the narrative of the times.
The Cabal.

Remember Julius Caesar purportedly burnt down the Great Library of Alexandria, Egypt. Losing 40,000 to 400,000 papyrus scrolls, equivalent to 100,000 rare books of Knowledge and Learning. Though a much smaller library survived called the Temple of Serapis.

Remember the Vatican hide many Truths under its grounds. They took 70,000 artifacts from Egypt, but only display 20,000. Why? The rest are hidden from the public. Why would the Vatican take Egyptian artifacts and hide them from us?

Remember Truths have been erased and hidden to keep the Human Race under control, indoctrinated and subservient to the Powers of our World Leaders. We are looked upon as slaves and lab rats to bring money to them and serve them.

Remember NASA own the rights to some of the Giza Plateau and the Egyptian Pyramids.

Remember to investigate the Moon landing, not what they put out there on MSM. Delve into it through the many other platforms available to you.

Remember we are not allowed to tour around Antarctica. We are only allowed to tour the outskirts. Who owns the World?

Remember there are hundreds of thousands of Children going missing every year, where do they go?

Remember some Children that go missing are still alive, sex trafficked, tortured, used for breeding and organ harvesting.

Linda M Noon

Food For Thought

Remember Chemtrails, Geo-engineering and Weather Manipulation. Rain, Snow, Floods and Droughts, Hurricanes and Earthquakes can be manmade. As our technology evolves, so does destruction and greed, under the guise of evolution and what the World Leaders say will be of great benefit for the Planet and all the inhabitants, apparently to make your life safer and easier.

Remember it is widely believed this Planet is overpopulated and we now have a Climate Change Crisis.

Remember there are many rich countries, with valuable resources, yet their own people are dying from sickness, starvation and homelessness. Including Australia.

Remember thousands upon thousands of Rain Forests are destroyed by man for their resources and land, leading to many species of animals losing their lives and natural habitats.

Remember we need trees to live, they take in what we breathe out and we breathe in what they release.

Remember we also need Bees to pollinate our plants.

Remember our Oceans are polluted and our marine life is killed by our disrespect, arrogance, negligence of plastics, waste and toxic chemicals.

Remember every living creature has a right to life.

Open Your Mind

Remember we cannot manifest in this dimension, the physical, without Action, usually beginning with a thought and the desire.

(You want a driver's license, you have to take action and learn to drive. You want to eat, you need to take action and get up and make it. You want a good job, you need the qualifications. To manifest a book you need to write it. As you strive towards your goal, synchronicities appear to take you in the direction of manifesting.)

Remember Intuition = In-tuition, inner guidance, lessons or Teachings. Gut reaction, following your heart.

Remember Imagination = Image In

Remember Integration = Balance of Mind and Body. Equilibrium.

Remember Duality. When one is out of balance a battle begins inside. We experience this both on a personal scale and at the moment a Worldwide scale. Has a lot to do with Emotions and thoughts. Programming.

(When one cannot make a decision either way, along comes the grey bit. Avoiding a decision leads to non action, confusion, procrastination, stress or depression. Not trusting your decision or being forced to make a decision that goes against what you feel is the right one for you, tips the balance again. I'm not talking about compromising; I am talking about your very own personal decisions. Peace-War, Love-Fear, Good-Bad, Yes-No, Can-Can't, I will-I won't, Up-Down, Black-White.)

Remember labelling yourself as an Empath is not the same as being Empathetic.

(Empaths take on other's pain and negativity, this leads them to judge others and label them energy vampires. This is a misconception as the Empath is also being an energy vampire for taking on the person's negativity. Empaths lack Emotional Intelligence and need to strengthen their own emotional reactions, by acknowledging it is not theirs, they do not want it and need to heal their own traumas. They are too emotionally charged, which can lead to melt downs. Meditation helps to strengthen the emotional body, forgiveness, compassion and Love. Imagine if Jesus was an Empath, he would not have healed the way he did, he would have been a mess, but he embodied Emotional Intelligence, where he remained Empathetic and Compassionate without taking on pain. The stronger your energy field, the less likely the negative impact on you. As the Empath heals and faces their own shadow, the less they will absorb this unwanted energy.
Raise your Vibration!)

Remember in our embodiment God, Christ, Buddha, and Krishna are within you, it is a Frequency and Vibration that we have given a label to and taken literally that they are better, more powerful than us. It has been written in the Holy Books.

(No one comes to the Father but by me, could this mean - INTERGRATION. I am the Father and you are in me, and I am in you, and you did not choose me, but I chose you. Could this mean - to physically live through you? You will seek me and shall not find me. Could this mean - we won't find him by looking outside of ourselves? Where I am you cannot come! Could this mean - because we are already there? This that I do, you also can do, if not better. Why look for the dead amongst the living?)

Remember you won't find Christ inside a book nor inside a building, because it is within you, you won't find anything outside of your embodiment.

Remember all Sages of the past Meditated within.

Remember this is not about any Religious Indoctrination created for putting the fear of God into you.

Remember when you pray, you are always asking for something outside of yourself. Sometimes in desperation. Instead send Blessings and Love. Bless your loved ones and your enemies.

Remember the way out is to go within, Meditate on stillness, Surrender, let go of any expectations and need for control. Let go of Ego. Open your mind.

Remember you are your own Guru, practice daily for at least twenty minutes to begin with. Soft music, sit up, with your spine straight, feet flat on the floor, if you can sit in the Lotus position, that's fine too. No lying down because it is too easy to fall asleep and you will have very little success on mastering the art of stilling the mind.

Remember stilling the mind is not easy but can be done, the mind will still chatter in the background but you will eventually be able to refrain from attaching to any given thought.

Remember to focus on the inside of your forehead, just above and in between the eyes, (3rd eye) like you are looking at a screen, just look there, watch what happens. At first you may feel uncomfortable in your body, aches, heat, chills, itches etc. but this is the Ego trying to sabotage you because it does not like change, it has had control of you your whole life. At some point you will begin to see swirling colours, maybe faces or landscapes or receive downloads of higher knowledge and wisdom.

Remember slowly and subtly over time, you will begin to see things differently, you will be able to control your emotions, you will feel more peaceful and happier. You will feel stronger and more in control as you allow your brain to release feel-good hormones naturally and become more positive.

Remember you are the boss of your own mind. The more you practice the easier it will be and the longer you can sit in this bliss. You will notice over time, things that used to bother you, no longer do. If they do it will be short lived, the changes come on subtly.

Remember you will begin to know things that you never thought about before, because it is all within.

Remember there are other guided forms of Meditation and they are good for stress but also a distraction from what you desire to achieve in your own awakening.

Remember your Pineal gland cannot be calcified, if that was so, all other organs would calcify too. The Pineal gland is tiny and made of Crystal Calcite, this is your antenna. It sits in the centre of your brain.

Remember to Respect everyone and everything until you have just cause not to. Then just walk away. You don't earn Respect. Unless you have stuffed up and need to make amends to rebuild it with another.

Remember never Trust or rely on anyone but yourself. Expect nothing from anyone. That way you cannot be let down by your expectations of another. But you can be pleasantly surprised.

Remember the shift into 5D is not about leaving 3D, it's about embracing the light within and living in that frequency.

Remember the eyes do not see, they collect data. The Brain sees, the Brain projects the hologram.

Remember the instant you look at someone's eyes for the first time, you can pick up a lot, if it feels off it usually is. This is discernment and intuition without judgement. Don't ignore it. Just be careful.

Remember not everyone will be a true friend and that's okay. Don't take it on board.

Remember to work on your shadow self. Trauma you may have experienced as a child needs to be forgiven, not matter what it was. This is a different approach from stillness Meditation. The more you push it down the darker it will be. Speak to your inner child, love it, embrace it, forgive it and dissolve it into your heart. This may be ongoing but gets easier over time, to the point the memory will always be there but once great healing begins you will no longer experience the pain and emotion of it and any physical pain or illness will subside.

Remember to White Sage Smudge your home on a regular basis, cleanse your space and bring it to a higher vibration, you cannot kill energy only transform it. Use tuning forks, Tibetan bells, diffuse 100% essential oils.

Remember do not play with Ouija boards, they have the potential to open you up to all kinds of Spiritual and physical mayhem.

Remember to talk kindly to yourself and about yourself, this will break any negative thoughts and habits and help to reprogram your mind.

Remember positive emotions relax DNA and cause it to unwind, to a point where it will create healing or create a new strand. Negative emotions cause it to tighten.

Remember your reality only exists where the mind focuses. If you think negative or lack then that will be your reality, if you think and feel Love, compassion and abundance that will be your reality. Where the mind goes energy flows.

Remember balance the Mind/Brain. Left Brain is Masculine, Right Brain is Feminine, when one is more dominant you will see imbalance. Meditate on inner stillness, calm the mind.

Remember to Meditate on your Heart as it has a mind of its own. There are around 40,000 neuron cells in your physical heart that think independently, the same as the cells in your brain but they don't communicate much. The Heart Neurons are 50,000 times more powerful than Left/Right Brain polarities, both magnetically and electrically. This was discovered in 1991. (Greg Baden)

Remember to begin your meditation with hand on heart to achieve the Heart/Brain connection, breath through your nose. When you desire to manifest before you come out of your meditation, begin with the outcome, feel the feeling/emotion, speak to the field as though it is already answered and give Thanks.

Remember to meditate on Heart, Brain/Mind connection. This way we can unify and use the Power within, connecting to your Christ self. Sacred Union. Heart Intelligence. Heart speaks to the brain, tells it what chemicals to release. Feelings of appreciation, gratitude and compassion will tell the brain the correct chemicals to release. Hand on heart, feel the feelings.

Remember when you achieve the connection to your Christ self, we as a whole (meaning the masses of humanity) will become a collective mass Christ Consciousness. This will create the second coming of Christ within us.

Remember we are our own Saviours. Waste no time, attention or energy waiting for a Saviour to come. Once all humanity achieves this state of being, watch the darkness lift.

Remember the darkness of the room disappears when you put a light on, you are that light.

Remember do not listen or believe everything you are told, do your research and find the truth within.

Remember man has been controlled and lied to by Darkness, it is not enough for us to know the Truth and to continue only knowing, this will not bring you to the light within. We have to find it within, nurture it, embody it and reflect it outwards into the darkness.

Remember we have been disempowered and separated from the Truth within, now is the time to take our power back.

Remember to act out of Love for Humanity, to be your true self.

Remember to allow healing to take place by forgiveness. Forgive often, every day, be it big or small. Forgiveness means to truly let go of the pain in your heart and mind. Hold no grudge. If you continually bring it back to you and feel the same pain over and over, then you have not forgiven.

Remember your energy field grows in strength and balance when you are embodying and vibrating unconditional Love.

Remember this World needs you as much as you need it, your Children from the Future need your love, guidance and knowledge.

Remember you have God encoded inside your DNA. All you need to do is activate it to remember who you are. No amount of money or possessions can give you that which you already are.

Remember to laugh a lot, dance, sing or cry, you have free will. Don't forget your inner child.

Remember when or if things seem hard, change your thought process towards whatever seems hard. Your mind believes what you say to it. Become aware of your thoughts and change them every time you catch yourself thinking negatively. Break the cycle and the habit, even if someone has verbally abused you, do not believe their words.

Remember you are so much more than you think you are.

Remember do not play negative scenarios over and over in your head. Forgive and let it go. Forgiveness isn't about going to a person and saying "I forgive you." When you don't, it comes from within. Forgive yourself as well. Miracles will take place in your physical, emotional and mental body too. You will know when you have done it because you will no longer carry the pain around, you will still have the memory, but no pain or reaction toward it. This is part of the Shadow work.

Remember when you meditate on inner stillness, where the mind is still and you become nothing, nothing but consciousness. You become the calm in the eye of the storm. Both inwardly and outwardly.

Remember do not fall for false spiritual guides unless you know Discernment and use it every single time by the power of three. Better still, stay within. Everything is within.

Remember we are all one. We have all been indoctrinated, programmed, lied to and misled. There are billions walking upon this Earth with minds set in this way, through no fault of their own. There are many waking up and freeing themselves, scrambling for information, proof and TRUTH like headless chickens. There are those who have managed to deprogram and see everything for what it is, and yet it still feels like we are getting nowhere, but we are, the TRUTH is coming to the surface like an old sunken ship being raised from the ocean bed and the most important thing is, it is all about the Children and their future.

Remember this book is to serve a purpose for the upcoming younger generations, as fore warned is fore armed.

Remember Individually you are but a grain of sand, collectively we are the Beach. You are a drop in the Ocean, collectively we are the Oceans. You are a blade of Grass, collectively we are the never ending Green Landscapes. You are a leaf on a tree, collectively we are the Forests. You are a breath of Air, collectively we are the Sky. You are a spec of Dust, collectively we are the Universe.
You are a micro within the macro.
Never forget who you Truly are.

Remember you tire as I tire, you weep as I weep, you bleed as I bleed, you wake as I wake, you strive as I strive, you burn as I burn, you rise as I rise, you Love as I Love.
You remember as I remember.

REMEMBER you are LIGHT.
Remember! Remember!
Wake Up and Remember!
Who you are.

Linda M Noon

Do You Remember?

More TRUTHS That I Have REMEMBERED...

_____
_____
_____
_____
_____
_____
_____
_____
_____
_____
_____
_____
_____
_____
_____
_____

Remember

I Remember...

I Remember...

I Remember...

I Remember...

I Remember...

I Remember...

I Remember...

I Remember...

I Remember...

I Remember...

I Remember...

I Remember...

Remember

The TRUTH will set you FREE!

Linda M Noon

Bibliography

Carson, Billy
The Emerald Tablets of Thoth

Website:
www.4biddenknowledge.com

YouTube:
@ForbiddenKnowledge1

Search Amazon for:
Emerald Tablets Billy Carson

Danaan, Elena
The Seeders - Return of the Gods
The True History of Earth, Mysteries of Ancient Space Arks & the Secret Hall of Records 2022

Website:
www.elenadanaan.org

YouTube:
@ElenaDanaan

Search Amazon for:
Elena-Danaan

Icke, David
The Answer
First publication August 2020 Iconic Publishing
Book about changing your perception of life and the World and set you free of the Illusions that control Human Society.

Website:
https://davidicke.com

Videos:
https://davidicke.com/category/videos/

Search Amazon for:
David Icke

Lipton, Bruce
The Biology of Belief
2005 Hay House Publishing
Unleashing the Power of Consciousness, Matter & Miracles

Search Amazon for:
Bruce Lipton

Reuckert, Carla L
The Law of One
Channeling series of a Higher Collective Consciousness. We are all One!

Search Amazon for:
Carla Rueckert

Noon, Linda M
The Awakening of the Lotus ~
First Published 2020 Lulu.com
Spiritual gifts & stories leading up to the
awakening of the Covid-19 and
misinformation. Finding Truth within.

Search Amazon for:
Linda M Noon

Noon, Linda M
Tilly's Journey to Fairy Kingdom ~
First Publication 2021 Lulu.com
Children's Book Fairy Tale.

Search Lulu.com for:
Linda Noon

Salla, Dr Michael
US Army Insider Missions
Galactic Federations Councils
JFK's Last Stand
and 6 other great books about the Truth
that is being deliberately concealed from us.

Website:
https://exopolitics.org

YouTube:
@MichaelSalla

Search Amazon for:
Dr Michael Salla

Websites & Social Media to explore:

- Bitchute.com
- GB News
- Newtube
- Patreon
- Rumble.com
- Turning Point
- Truthsocial.com
- Youtube

Facebook Groups:

- Aussies Against Lockdown
- SGA
- Died Suddenly Australia
- We Are In This Together
- Café Locked Out
- We the people of Australia
- Let Freedom Ring
- TRS and Safe Heavy Metals Detox
- Lifewave X39 Stem Cell Patches Melb

Politicians & Senators:

- Pauline Hanson (One Nation)
- Senator Malcolm Roberts (One Nation)
- Bernie Finn (Family First)
- Senator Alex Antic (SA Liberal Party)
- David Limbrick MP (Liberal Democrats)
- Senator Babet (United Australia Party)

Acknowledgments

To all the People, Insightful Meditations, Dreams & Downloads that inspired me to write this Book, especially my Grand Children.

Thank you to my Grand Children for your presence in my life and your little one-liner questions here and there, that activated within me and set the wheels in motion to discover some answers for you. To hopefully make yours and other Children's Journey through this life that little more easier. To sift the Wheat from the Chaff. Bullshit baffles Brains.

Thank you to Michael Young, an Author & Editor for encouraging me and always listening to my way-out thoughts and teachings. For your kindness towards myself and others.

To Janelle Jordon & Michael Young both for taking the weekly Journeys we travel together, in and out of Dimensions.

Thank you to my Family, especially my Sons and Daughter-In-Law for always accepting me just the way I am, as well as making fun of me at times. (Without me your life would be boring).

Thank you to my Best Friend Sheila Warne for putting up with my craziness, who sometimes tells me, "No one else, would think of that shit, except you." Only because of some of the thoughts I share aloud with her, because I can, and all of my other Friends for your social presence in my life.

What an amazing Journey!

Linda M Noon

Remember

About the Author

Linda M Noon

Has been on a Spiritual Journey of more than 25 years trying to discover the meaning of Life, Truth & Enlightenment. Going through many years of Personal Meditation & Spiritual Growth. As well as, along the way Studying with a Senior Abbott Buddhist Monk for 3 years. Venerable Master Thang.

Born in Salford, North England, now living in Melbourne, Victoria Australia. The Author throughout her life always had questions and always wanted to know the Truth about the intangible existence of other Worldly realities or unrealities. One of the main questions has been "What if everything we think we know in our world, is not true?" Memorise and repeat.

This book gives food for thought, to not follow blindly what one hears, sees or is enforced upon them, but to question, discern and investigate. Listen carefully to the contradictions bombarded upon you. Watch the actions of man. Follow your Heart. This book is a ship in the night, guiding you into still waters of safety, light and truth. You are Light and only Light.

Linda M Noon

The Author:

- ➤ Author and Poet
- ➤ Meditation Teacher 26 yrs. Going within.
- ➤ Clinical Hypnotherapist Dip.Clin.Hyp 20 yrs. *Now retired.*
- ➤ Reiki Master/Teacher 27 yrs. *Now retired.*

Published books:

The Awakening of the Lotus
on lulu.com

Tilly's Journey to Fairy Kingdom
on lulu.com and Amazon

Email: chambersoflight@outlook.com

A proud Mother & Grand Mother, who also enjoys Art & Crafts, Nature, Animals & Road Trips.

Remember

www.ingramcontent.com/pod-product-compliance
Lightning Source LLC
LaVergne TN
LVHW010308070426
835510LV00025B/3413